step-by-step

potatoes

p

This is a Parragon Book
First published in 2002

Parragon
Queen Street House
4 Queen Street
Bath BA1 1HE
United Kingdom

ISBN: 0-75258-007-8

Printed in Spain

Produced by The Bridgewater Book Company Ltd, Lewes, East Sussex

Acknowledgements
Creative Director Terry Jeavons
Art Director Sarah Howerd
Editorial Director Fiona Biggs
Senior Editor Mark Truman
Editorial Assistants Simon Bailey, Tom Kitch
Page Make-up Chris Akroyd

NOTES FOR THE READER

- This book uses both metric and imperial measurements. Follow the same units of measurement throughout; do not mix metric and imperial.
- All spoon measurements are level: teaspoons are assumed to be 5 ml, and tablespoons are assumed to be 15 ml.
- Unless otherwise stated, milk is assumed to be full-fat, eggs and individual vegetables such as potatoes are medium-sized, and pepper is freshly ground black pepper.
- Recipes using raw or very lightly cooked eggs should be avoided by infants, the elderly, pregnant women, convalescents, and anyone suffering from an illness.
- Optional ingredients, variations, and serving suggestions have not been included in the calculations.
- The times given are an approximate guide only. Preparation times differ according to the techniques used by different people and the cooking times vary as a result of the type of oven used.

Contents

Introduction

Potatoes are perhaps the most versatile of all vegetables. Not only can they be served in a wide variety of ways to accompany a main course but they can also be an integral part of a main course. A vegetable, meat or fish base, topped with mashed potatoes and cheese and baked in the oven until crisp and golden, makes a wonderful homely and comforting dish. Potatoes add just the right amount of body to a smooth soup and contribute a satisfying chunkiness to a thick, hearty soup. New potatoes are delicious boiled and then cooled to use in a salad. They can even be transformed into a base to be used as an alternative to a dough base for a pizza. Potato & Pepperoni Pizza is ideal for pizza lovers who have a gluten intolerance.

There are many varieties of potato, so always select a suitable potato for a dish you plan to cook. Be guided by the ingredients

guide to recipe key	
easy	Recipes are graded as follows: 1 pea = easy; 2 peas = very easy; 3 peas = extremely easy.
serves 4	Most of the recipes in this book serve four people. Simply halve the ingredients to serve two, taking care not to mix imperial and metric measurements.
15 minutes	Preparation time. Where recipes include soaking, standing, or poaching, times for these are listed separately: eg, 15 minutes, plus 30 minutes to stand.
15 minutes	Cooking time. Cooking times do not include the cooking of rice, noodles or vegetables served with the main dishes.

list that accompanies each recipe. Waxy potatoes hold their shape during cooking – when sliced and cooked on top of a hotpot or a pie, or when fried for a Spanish tortilla. Floury potatoes soften while cooking, so they are ideal for mashing to use as a topping and for binding fishcakes or nut roasts. They also absorb other flavours readily, so they are perfect for spicy dishes, such as Spicy Potato & Rice Pilaf or Indian Potato Salad. Sweet potatoes may be served with savoury dishes or teamed with bananas to make a deliciously different warm Sweet Potato & Banana Salad, with a honey, lemon and chive dressing.

Potato, Sausage & Onion Pie, page 44

Soups

Potatoes appear in many classic soup recipes. An old favourite is leek & potato soup or Vichyssoise, which may be served hot or chilled. An interesting variation of this is Celeriac, Leek & Potato Soup. Celeriac is a knobbly root vegetable which may look unpromising, but has a subtle celery flavour. Another classic to be found in the following pages is Cullen Skink from Scotland. 'Skink' means 'soup', and this is a thick, creamy fish soup made from cod and smoked haddock. It is warming and satisfying, but also luxurious.

Celeriac, Leek & Potato Soup

INGREDIENTS

25 g/1 oz butter
1 onion, chopped
2 large leeks, halved
*   lengthways and*
*   sliced*
1 large celeriac (about
*   750 g/1 lb 10 oz),*
*   peeled and cubed*
1 potato, cubed
1 carrot, quartered and
*   sliced thinly*
1.2 litres/2 pints water
⅛ tsp dried marjoram
1 bay leaf
freshly grated nutmeg
salt and pepper
celery leaves, to garnish

❶ Melt the butter in a large saucepan over a medium–low heat. Add the onion and leeks and cook for about 4 minutes, stirring frequently, until just softened; do not allow to colour.

❷ Add the celeriac, potato, carrot, water, marjoram and bay leaf, and a large pinch of salt. Bring to the boil, reduce the heat, cover, and simmer for about 25 minutes until the vegetables are tender. Remove the bay leaf.

❸ Allow the soup to cool slightly. Transfer to a blender or a food processor and purée until smooth. (If using a food processor, strain off the cooking liquid and reserve. Purée the soup solids with enough cooking liquid to moisten them, then combine with remaining liquid.)

❹ Return the puréed soup to the saucepan and stir to blend in the ingredients. Season with salt, pepper and nutmeg. Simmer over a medium–low heat until reheated.

❺ Ladle the soup into warm bowls, garnish with celery leaves, and serve.

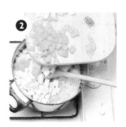

 very easy

 serves 4

 15 minutes

 45 minutes

Roasted Garlic & Potato Soup

INGREDIENTS

1 large bulb of garlic with large cloves, peeled (about 100 g/3½ oz)
2 tsp olive oil
2 large leeks, sliced thinly
1 large onion, chopped finely
3 potatoes, diced (about 500 g/1 lb 2 oz)
1.2 litres/2 pints chicken or vegetable stock
1 bay leaf
150 ml/5 fl oz light cream
freshly grated nutmeg
fresh lemon juice (optional)
salt and pepper
snipped fresh chives or parsley, to garnish

❶ Put the garlic cloves on a baking sheet, brush lightly with oil, and bake in a preheated oven at 180°C/350°F/Gas Mark 4 for about 20 minutes until golden.

❷ Heat the oil in a large saucepan over a medium heat. Add the leeks and onion, cover, and cook for about 3 minutes, stirring frequently, until they begin to soften.

❸ Add the potatoes, roasted garlic, stock and bay leaf. Season as necessary with salt and pepper. Bring to the boil, reduce the heat, cover the pan, and cook the soup gently for about 30 minutes until the vegetables are tender. Remove the bay leaf.

❹ Allow the soup to cool slightly, then transfer it to a blender or a food processor and purée until smooth, working in batches if necessary. (If using a food processor, strain off the cooking liquid and reserve. Purée the soup solids with enough cooking liquid to moisten them, then combine with the remaining liquid.)

❺ Return the soup to the saucepan and stir in the cream and a generous grating of nutmeg. Taste and adjust the seasoning, if necessary, adding a few drops of lemon juice, to taste. Rewarm over a low heat. Ladle into warm soup bowls, garnish with chives or parsley, and serve.

 very easy

 serves 4

 10 minutes

 1 hour

Sweet Potato, Apple & Leek Soup

INGREDIENTS

12.5 g/½ oz butter
3 leeks, sliced thinly
1 large carrot, sliced
    thinly
2 sweet potatoes,
    peeled and cubed
2 large tart apples, such
    as Granny Smiths,
    peeled and cubed
    (about 600 g/1 lb 5 oz)
1.3 litres/2 pints water
freshly grated nutmeg
225 ml/8 fl oz apple
    juice
225 ml/8 fl oz whipping
    cream
salt and pepper
snipped fresh chives or
    coriander leaves,
    to garnish

❶ Melt the butter in a large saucepan over a medium-low heat. Add the leeks, cover the pan, and cook for 6–8 minutes, or until softened, stirring frequently.

❷ Add the carrot, sweet potatoes, apples and water. Season with salt, pepper and nutmeg. Bring to the boil, reduce the heat, and simmer, covered, for about 20 minutes, or until the vegetables are tender, stirring occasionally.

❸ Allow the soup to cool slightly, then transfer to a blender or a food processor and purée until smooth, working in batches if necessary. (If using a food processor, strain off the cooking liquid and reserve. Purée the soup solids with enough cooking liquid to moisten them, then combine with the remaining liquid.)

❹ Return the puréed soup to the saucepan and stir in the apple juice. Place over a low heat and simmer for about 10 minutes until heated through.

❺ Stir in the cream and continue simmering for about 5 minutes, stirring frequently, until heated through. Taste and adjust the seasoning, adding more salt, pepper and nutmeg, if necessary. Ladle the soup into warm bowls, garnish with chives or coriander, and serve.

 very easy

 serves 4

10 minutes

45 minutes

Smoked Haddock & Potato Soup

INGREDIENTS

1 tbsp oil
55 g/2 oz bacon, cut
   into thin strips
1 large onion, chopped
   finely
2 tbsp plain flour
1 litre/1¾ pints milk
700 g/1 lb 9 oz
   potatoes, cut into
   1.2 cm/½ inch cubes
175 g/6 oz skinless
   smoked haddock
salt and pepper
fresh parsley, chopped
   finely, to garnish

❶ Heat the oil in a large saucepan over a medium heat. Add the bacon and cook for 2 minutes. Stir in the onion and continue cooking for 5–7 minutes, stirring frequently, until the onion is soft and the bacon golden. Tip the pan and spoon off as much fat as possible.

❷ Stir in the flour and continue cooking for 2 minutes. Add half of the milk and stir well, scraping the bottom of the pan to mix in the flour.

❸ Add the potatoes and remaining milk and season with pepper. Bring just to the boil, stirring frequently. Reduce the heat and simmer, partially covered, for 10 minutes.

❹ Add the fish and continue cooking, stirring occasionally, for about 15 minutes, or until the potatoes are tender and the fish breaks up easily.

❺ Taste the soup and adjust the seasoning (salt may not be needed). Ladle into a warm tureen or bowls, and sprinkle generously with chopped parsley.

 very easy

 serves 4

 5–10 minutes

 40 minutes

COOK'S TIP

Cutting the potatoes into small cubes not only looks attractive but it also allows them to cook more quickly and evenly.

Spicy Potato & Chickpea Soup

INGREDIENTS

1 tbsp olive oil
1 large onion, chopped finely
2–3 garlic cloves, chopped finely or crushed
1 carrot, quartered and sliced thinly
350 g/12 oz potatoes, diced
¼ tsp ground turmeric
¼ tsp garam masala
¼ tsp mild curry powder
400 g/14 oz can chopped tomatoes in juice
850 ml/1½ pints water
¼ tsp chilli purée, or to taste
400 g/14 oz can chickpeas, rinsed and drained
85 g/3 oz fresh or frozen peas
salt and pepper
chopped fresh coriander, to garnish

❶ Heat the olive oil in a large saucepan over a medium heat. Add the onion and garlic, and cook for 3–4 minutes, stirring occasionally, until the onion is beginning to soften.

❷ Add the carrot, potatoes, turmeric, garam masala and curry powder, and continue to cook cook for 1–2 minutes.

❸ Add the tomatoes, water and chilli purée, and a large pinch of salt. Reduce the heat, cover and simmer for 30 minutes, stirring occasionally.

❹ Add the chickpeas and peas to the pan, and continue cooking for about 15 minutes, or until all the vegetables are tender.

❺ Taste the soup and adjust the seasoning, if necessary, adding a little more chilli if wished. Ladle into warm soup bowls and sprinkle with coriander.

 very easy

 serves 4

 5 minutes

 50 minutes

Green Lentil, Potato & Ham Soup

INGREDIENTS

300 g/10½ oz Puy lentils
6 g/¼ oz butter
1 large onion, chopped
   finely
2 carrots, chopped finely
1 garlic clove, chopped
450 ml/16 fl oz water
1 bay leaf
¼ tsp dried sage or
   rosemary
1 litre/1 ¾ pints chicken
   stock
225 g/8 oz potatoes,
   diced
1 tbsp tomato purée
115 g/4 oz smoked ham,
   diced finely
salt and pepper
chopped fresh parsley,
   to garnish

 very easy

serves 5

10–15 minutes

45 minutes

❶ Rinse and drain the lentils and check for any small stones.

❷ Melt the butter in a large saucepan or a flameproof casserole over a medium heat. Add the onion, carrots, and garlic, cover the pan, and cook for 4–5 minutes, or until the onion is slightly softened, stirring frequently.

❸ Add the lentils to the vegetables with the water, bay leaf and sage or rosemary. Bring the pan to the boil, reduce the heat, cover, and simmer for 10 minutes.

❹ Add the stock, potatoes, tomato purée and ham. Bring back to a simmer. Cover and continue simmering for 25–30 minutes, or until the vegetables are tender.

❺ Season to taste with salt and pepper, and remove the bay leaf. Ladle the soup into warm bowls, garnish with parsley, and serve hot.

COOK'S TIP

Cut the potatoes into small cubes, about 5mm/¼ inch, so they will be in proportion to the lentils.

Cullen Skink

INGREDIENTS

225 g/8 oz smoked
   haddock fillet
25 g/1 oz butter
1 onion, chopped finely
600 ml/1 pint milk
350 g/12 oz potatoes,
   diced
350 g/12 oz cod, boned,
   skinned and cubed
150 ml/5 fl oz double
   cream
2 tbsp chopped fresh
   parsley
lemon juice, to taste
salt and pepper

TO GARNISH
lemon slices
parsley sprigs

 very easy

 serves 4

 20 minutes

 35 minutes,
   plus 10 minutes
   to poach

COOK'S TIP
Rather than use
yellow-dyed haddock
fillet, which may be
whiting and not
haddock at all, look
for Finnan haddock.

❶ Put the haddock fillet in a large frying pan and cover with boiling water. Leave for 10 minutes. Drain, reserving 300 ml/10 fl oz of the soaking water. Flake the fish, taking care to remove all the bones.

❷ Heat the butter in a large saucepan and add the onion. Cook gently for 10 minutes until softened. Add the milk and bring to a slow simmer, then add the potato and cook it gently for 10 minutes.

❸ Add the reserved haddock flakes and the cod. Simmer for another 10 minutes until the cod is tender.

❹ Remove about one-third of the fish and potatoes, put in a food processor, and blend until smooth. Alternatively, push through a sieve into a bowl. Return to the soup with the cream, parsley, and seasoning. Taste and add a little lemon juice, if desired. Add a little of the reserved soaking water if the soup seems too thick. Reheat gently and serve at once, garnished with lemon slices and parsley sprigs.

New England Clam Chowder

INGREDIENTS

900 g/2 lb live clams
4 slices rindless streaky
* bacon, chopped*
25 g/1 oz butter
1 onion, chopped
1 tbsp chopped fresh
* thyme*
1 large potato, diced
300 ml/10 fl oz milk
1 bay leaf
150 ml/10 fl oz cream
salt and pepper
1 tbsp chopped fresh
* parsley*
reserve 8 clams in their
* shells, to garnish*
* (see Cook's Tip)*

 easy

serves 4

 15 minutes

30 minutes

COOK'S TIP
A smart way of presenting this dish is to sit 2 of the reserved clams in their shells on top of each bowl of soup just before serving.

❶ Scrub the clams and put into a large saucepan with a splash of water. Cook over a high heat for 3–4 minutes until all the clams have opened. Discard any that remain closed. Strain the clams, reserving the cooking liquid. Set aside until cool enough to handle.

❷ Remove the clams from their shells, chop them coarsely if they are large, and set aside.

❸ In a clean saucepan fry the bacon until browned and crisp. Drain on kitchen paper. Add the butter to the same pan and when it has melted, add the onion. Cook for 4–5 minutes until softened but not coloured. Add the thyme and cook briefly before adding the potato, the reserved clam cooking liquid, the milk and the bay leaf. Bring to the boil and simmer for 10 minutes, or until the potato is just tender.

❹ Transfer to a food processor and blend until smooth, or push through a sieve into a bowl.

❺ Add the reserved clams, the bacon and cream. Simmer for 2–3 minutes until heated through. Season, stir in the parsley, and serve, garnished with clams in their shells.

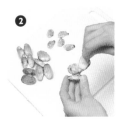

22

Main Meals

If meals based on potatoes conjure up an image of snacks and midweek suppers, the recipes in this section will give you plenty of ideas for converting them into elegant starters and main-course dishes for weekend lunches and dinners. Veal Italienne is a casserole cooked with the perennially popular ingredients of Italian cuisine – red wine, tomatoes, olives and basil. For a special potato dish to serve vegetarian guests, try Potato-Topped Vegetables in Wine. The distinctive flavour of fennel in the base is echoed by fennel seeds in the cheese and potato topping.

Quick Chicken Bake

*500 g/1 lb 2 oz minced
    chicken
1 large onion, chopped
    finely
2 carrots, diced finely
25 g/1 oz plain flour
1 tbsp tomato purée
300 ml/10 fl oz
    chicken stock
pinch of fresh thyme
900 g/2 lb potatoes,
    cooked and mashed
    with butter and milk,
    and highly seasoned
90 g/3 oz grated
    Lancashire cheese
salt and pepper
peas, to serve*

❶ Dry-fry the minced chicken, onion and carrots in a non-stick pan for 5 minutes to brown them, stirring frequently.

❷ Sprinkle the chicken with the flour and simmer for another 2 minutes.

❸ Gradually blend in the tomato purée and stock, then simmer for 15 minutes. Season and add the thyme.

❹ Transfer the chicken and vegetable mixture to an ovenproof casserole and allow to cool.

❺ Spoon the mashed potato over the chicken mixture and sprinkle with the Lancashire cheese. Bake in a preheated oven, 200°C/400°F/Gas Mark 6, for 20 minutes, or until the cheese is bubbling and golden. Serve hot with the peas.

 very easy

 serves 4

10 minutes,
plus 15 minutes
to cool

45 minutes

COOK'S TIP
Cotswold cheese, a blend of Double Gloucester, onion, and chives, makes a tasty alternative to Lancashire as a topping for this pie. Alternatively, use a mixture of cheeses.

Potato, Beef & Peanut Pot

INGREDIENTS

1 tbsp vegetable oil
60 g/2 oz butter
450 g/1 lb lean beef
  steak, cut into
  thin strips
1 onion, halved and
  sliced
2 garlic cloves, crushed
2 large waxy potatoes,
  cubed
½ tsp paprika
4 tbsp crunchy peanut
  butter
600 ml/1 pint beef stock
25 g/1 oz unsalted
  peanuts
2 tsp light soy sauce
50 g/1¾ oz sugar
  snap peas
1 red pepper, cut
  into strips
parsley sprigs,
  to garnish

❶ Heat the oil and butter in a flameproof casserole dish.

❷ Add the beef strips and fry them gently for 3–4 minutes, stirring and turning the meat until it is sealed on all sides.

❸ Add the onion and garlic and cook for another 2 minutes, stirring constantly.

❹ Add the potato cubes and cook for 3–4 minutes or until they begin to brown slightly.

❺ Stir in the paprika and peanut butter, then blend in the beef stock little by little. Bring the mixture to the boil, stirring frequently.

❻ Add the peanuts, soy sauce, sugar snap peas and red pepper to the pan.

❼ Cover and cook over a low heat for 45 minutes or until the beef is cooked through.

❽ Serve the dish hot, garnished with parsley sprigs, and accompanied by plain boiled rice or noodles.

 very easy

 serves 4

 5 minutes

 1 hour

Veal Italienne

INGREDIENTS

60 g/2 oz butter
1 tbsp olive oil
675 g/1½ lb potatoes,
    cubed
4 veal escalopes,
    weighing about
    175 g/6 oz each
1 onion, cut into
    8 wedges
2 garlic cloves, crushed
2 tbsp plain flour
2 tbsp tomato purée
150 ml/5 fl oz red wine
300 ml/10 fl oz
    chicken stock
8 ripe tomatoes, peeled,
    deseeded and diced
25 g/1 oz stoned black
    olives, halved
2 tbsp chopped fresh
    basil
salt and pepper
fresh basil leaves,
    to garnish

❶ Heat the butter and oil in a large frying pan. Add the potato cubes and cook for 5–7 minutes, stirring frequently, until they begin to brown.

❷ Remove the potatoes from the pan with a perforated spoon and set aside.

❸ Place the veal in the frying pan and cook for 2–3 minutes on each side until sealed. Remove from the pan and set aside.

❹ Add the onion and garlic to the pan and cook for 2–3 minutes.

❺ Add the flour and tomato purée and cook for 1 minute, stirring. Gradually blend in the red wine and chicken stock, stirring to make a smooth sauce.

❻ Return the potatoes and veal to the pan. Stir in the tomatoes, olives and chopped basil, and season with salt and pepper.

❼ Transfer to a casserole dish and cook in a preheated oven, 180°C/350°F/Gas Mark 4, for 1 hour or until the potatoes and veal are cooked through. Garnish with fresh basil leaves, and serve.

 very easy

 serves 4

 25 minutes

 1 hour
20 minutes

Lamb Hotpot

INGREDIENTS

675 g/1½ lb best end
of lamb neck cutlets
2 lamb's kidneys
675 g/1½ lb waxy
potatoes, scrubbed
and sliced thinly
1 large onion, sliced
thinly
2 tbsp chopped fresh
thyme
150 ml/ 5 fl oz lamb
stock
25 g/1 oz butter, melted
salt and pepper
fresh thyme sprigs,
to garnish

easy

serves 4

15 minutes

2 hours

❶ Remove any excess fat from the lamb. Skin and core the kidneys and cut them into slices.

❷ Arrange a layer of potatoes in the base of a 1.8 litre/ 3 pint ovenproof dish.

❸ Arrange the lamb neck cutlets on top of the potatoes and cover with the sliced kidneys, onion and chopped fresh thyme.

❹ Pour the lamb stock over the meat and season to taste with salt and pepper.

❺ Layer the remaining potato slices on top, overlapping to cover the meat and sliced onion completely.

❻ Brush the potato slices with the butter, cover the dish, and cook in a preheated oven, 180°C/350°F/Gas Mark 4, for 1½ hours.

❼ Remove the lid and cook for another 30 minutes until golden brown on top.

❽ Garnish with fresh thyme sprigs and serve hot.

COOK'S TIP
Oysters are tradition-
ally included in this
tasty hotpot. They
should be added to
each layer, along with
the kidneys.

Potato & Pepperoni Pizza

very easy

serves 4

20 minutes

45 minutes

❶ Grease and flour a 23 cm/9 inch pizza tin.

❷ Cook the diced potatoes in a saucepan of boiling water for 10 minutes or until cooked through. Drain and mash until smooth. Transfer the mashed potato to a mixing bowl and stir in the butter, garlic, herbs and egg.

❸ Spread the mixture into the prepared pizza pan. Cook in a preheated oven, 225°C/425°F/Gas Mark 7, for 7–10 minutes or until the pizza base begins to set.

❹ Mix the passata and tomato purée together and spoon it over the pizza base, to within 1 cm/½ inch of the edge of the base.

❺ Slice the pepperoni, and arrange it with the peppers, mushrooms and olives on top of the passata.

❻ Scatter the mozzarella cheese on top of the pizza. Cook in the oven for 20 minutes or until the base is cooked through and the cheese has melted on top. Serve the pizza hot with a mixed salad.

❸
❹
❻

Potato, Tomato & Sausage Pan-fry

INGREDIENTS

2 large potatoes, sliced
1 tbsp vegetable oil
8 flavoured sausages
1 red onion, cut into
    8 wedges
1 tbsp tomato purée
150 ml/5 fl oz red wine
150 ml/5 fl oz passata
2 large tomatoes, each
    cut into 8 wedges
175 g/6 oz broccoli
    florets, blanched
2 tbsp chopped fresh
    basil
salt and pepper
shredded fresh basil,
    to garnish

 very easy

 serves 4

5 minutes

30 minutes

COOK'S TIP
Broccoli adds a splash of colour to this dish, but other vegetables may be used. Canned plum tomatoes may be substituted for passata.

❶ Cook the sliced potatoes in a saucepan of boiling water for 7 minutes. Drain thoroughly and set aside.

❷ Meanwhile, heat the oil in a large frying pan. Add the sausages and cook for 5 minutes, turning the sausages frequently to ensure that they are browned on all sides.

❸ Add the onion pieces to the pan and continue to cook for another 5 minutes, stirring the mixture frequently.

❹ Stir in the tomato purée, the red wine and the passata, and mix well. Add the tomato wedges, broccoli florets and chopped basil to the panfry, and mix carefully.

❺ Add the parboiled potato slices to the pan. Cook the mixture for about 10 minutes, or until the sausages are cooked through. Season to taste with salt and pepper.

❻ Garnish the panfry with fresh shredded basil and serve hot, directly from the pan, or transfer to a serving plate before sprinkling with the garnish.

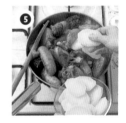

Creamy Chicken & Potato Casserole

INGREDIENTS

2 tbsp vegetable oil
60 g/2 oz butter
4 chicken portions, each
    about 225 g/8 oz
2 leeks, sliced
1 garlic clove, crushed
4 tbsp plain flour
900 ml/1½ pints
    chicken stock
300 ml/10 fl oz dry
    white wine
125 g/4½ oz baby
    carrots, halved
    lengthways
125 g/4½ oz baby
    sweetcorn cobs,
    halved lengthways
450 g/1 lb small new
    potatoes
1 bouquet garni
150 ml/5 fl oz double
    cream
salt and pepper

❶ Heat the oil and butter in a large frying pan. Cook the chicken portions for 10 minutes, turning until evenly browned. Transfer the chicken to a casserole dish using a perforated spoon.

❷ Add the leek and garlic to the frying pan and cook for 2–3 minutes, stirring. Stir in the flour and cook for another minute. Remove the frying pan from the heat and stir in the stock and wine. Season well.

❸ Return the pan to the heat and bring the mixture slowly to the boil. Stir in the carrots, sweetcorn and the potatoes, and add the bouquet garni.

❹ Transfer the mixture to the casserole dish. Cover and cook in a preheated oven, 180°C/350°F/Gas Mark 4, for about 1 hour.

❺ Remove the casserole from the oven and stir in the cream. Return the casserole uncovered to the oven, and cook for 15 minutes more. Remove the bouquet garni and discard. Adjust the seasoning to taste. Serve the casserole with plain rice and fresh vegetables, such as broccoli.

 very easy

 serves 4

 5 minutes

 1 hour
30 minutes

Potato, Beef & Leek Pasties

INGREDIENTS

225 g/8 oz waxy
  potatoes, diced
1 small carrot, diced
225 g/8 oz beef steak,
  cut into cubes
salt and pepper
1 leek, sliced
225 g/8 oz ready-made
  shortcrust pastry
15 g/ ½ oz butter
1 egg, beaten

 easy

 serves 4

 10–15 minutes

🕐 50 minutes

VARIATION
Use other types of
meat, such as pork or
chicken, in the pasties
and add chunks of
apple in step 2.

❶ Grease a baking sheet lightly.

❷ Mix the potatoes, carrots, beef and leek in a large bowl. Season well with salt and pepper.

❸ Divide the pastry into 4 equal portions. On a lightly floured surface, roll each portion into a 20 cm/8 inch round.

❹ Spoon the potato mixture along the centre of each round, to within 1 cm/½ inch of the edge. Top the mixture with the butter, dividing it equally between the rounds. Brush the pastry edge with a little of the beaten egg.

❺ Fold the pastry over to encase the filling and crimp the edges together.

❻ Transfer the pasties to the prepared baking sheet and brush them with the beaten egg.

❼ Bake in a preheated oven, 200°C/400°F/Gas Mark 6, for 20 minutes. Reduce the oven temperature to 160°C/325°F/Gas Mark 3, and bake the pasties for another 30 minutes until cooked.

❽ Serve the pasties with a crisp salad or with onion gravy.

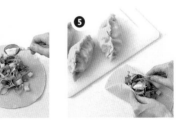

Carrot-topped Beef Pie

 very easy

 serves 4

 10 minutes

 1 hour 5 minutes

❶ Dry-fry the beef in a large pan set over a high heat for 3–4 minutes, or until the heat seals it. Add the onion and garlic, and cook for another 5 minutes, stirring.

❷ Add the flour and cook for 1 minute. Gradually blend in the beef stock and tomato purée. Stir in the celery, 1 tablespoon of the parsley, and the Worcestershire sauce. Season to taste with salt and pepper.

❸ Bring the mixture to the boil, then reduce the heat and simmer for 20–25 minutes. Spoon the beef mixture into a 1.1 litre/2 pint pie dish.

❹ Meanwhile, cook the potatoes and carrots in a saucepan of boiling water for 10 minutes. Drain them thoroughly and mash them, then stir the butter, milk, and the remaining parsley into the potato and carrot mixture, and season.

❺ Spoon the potato and carrot mixture on top of the beef mixture to cover it, completely. Alternatively, pipe it on using a piping bag.

❻ Cook the pie in a preheated oven, 190°C/375°F/Gas Mark 5, for 45 minutes or until cooked through. Serve hot.

Potato, Sausage & Onion Pie

INGREDIENTS

2 large waxy potatoes,
   unpeeled and sliced
25 g/1 oz/butter
4 thick pork and herb
   sausages
1 leek, sliced
2 garlic cloves, crushed
150 ml/5 fl oz vegetable
   stock
150 ml/5 fl oz dry cider
   or apple juice
2 tbsp chopped
   fresh sage
2 tbsp cornflour
4 tbsp water
75 g/2¾ oz mature
   cheese, grated
salt and pepper

very easy

serves 4

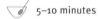

5–10 minutes

40 minutes

VARIATIONS

Other vegetables,
such as broccoli or
cauliflower, may be
added to the filling.
White wine may be
substituted for cider
or apple juice.

❶ Cook the sliced potatoes in a saucepan of boiling water for 10 minutes. Drain and set aside.

❷ Meanwhile, melt the butter in a frying pan and cook the sausages for 8–10 minutes, turning them frequently so that they brown on all sides. Remove the sausages from the pan and cut them into thick slices.

❸ Add the leek, garlic and sausage slices to the pan, and cook for 2–3 minutes.

❹ Add the vegetable stock, cider or apple juice and chopped sage to the pan. Season with salt and pepper. Blend the cornflour with the water, stir the mixture into the pan, and bring to the boil, stirring until the sauce is thick and clear. Spoon the mixture into a deep pie dish.

❺ Layer the potato slices on top of the sausage mixture to cover it completely. Season with salt and pepper, and sprinkle the grated cheese over the top.

❻ Cook in a preheated oven, 190°C/375°F/Gas Mark 5, for 25–30 minutes or until the potatoes are cooked and the cheese is golden brown. Serve the pie hot.

Smoked Fish Pie

INGREDIENTS

2 tbsp olive oil
1 onion, chopped finely
1 leek, sliced thinly
1 carrot, diced
1 stick of celery, diced
115 g/4o oz button
   mushrooms, halved
grated rind 1 lemon
350 g/12 oz skinless,
   boneless smoked
   cod fillet, cubed
350 g/12 oz skinless,
   boneless white
   fish, cubed
250 g/8 oz cooked
   peeled prawns
2 tbsp chopped parsley
1 tbsp chopped fresh dill
salt and pepper

SAUCE
30 g/1 oz butter
50 g/1¾ oz plain flour
1 tsp mustard powder
600 ml/1 pint milk
55 g/2 oz Gruyère
   cheese

TOPPING
675 g/1 lb 8 oz
   potatoes, unpeeled
55 g/2 oz butter, melted
25 g/1 oz Gruyère
   cheese, grated

❶ To make the sauce, melt the butter in a saucepan and add the flour and mustard. Stir until smooth and cook over a low heat for 2 minutes without colouring. Beat in the milk until smooth. Simmer for 2 minutes, then stir in the cheese until smooth. Remove from the heat. Stretch clingfilm over the surface of the sauce to prevent a skin forming. Set aside.

❷ Meanwhile, boil the potatoes for the topping in salted water for 15 minutes. Drain and set aside to cool.

❸ Heat the olive oil in a clean pan and add the onion. Cook for 5 minutes until softened. Add the leek, carrot, celery, and mushrooms, and cook for 10 minutes, or until the vegetables soften. Stir in the lemon rind and cook briefly.

❹ Add the vegetables, fish, prawns, parsley and dill to the pan, and season. Transfer to a greased casserole dish.

❺ Peel the cooled potatoes and grate them coarsely. Mix with the melted butter. Cover the filling with the grated potato, and grate Gruyère cheese over the top.

❻ Cover with foil, and bake in a preheated oven at 200°C/400°F/Gas Mark 6 for 30 minutes. Remove the foil and bake for 30 minutes more. Serve while the filling is still bubbling.

very easy

serves 4

35–40 minutes

1 hour 20 minutes

Herring & Potato Pie

1 tbsp Dijon mustard
115 g/4 oz butter,
    softened
450 g/1 lb herrings,
    filleted
750 g/1 lb 10 oz potatoes
1 large onion, sliced
2 cooking apples,
    sliced thinly
1 tsp chopped fresh sage
600 ml/1 pint hot
    fish stock
50 g/1¾ oz crustless
    ciabatta bread, made
    into breadcrumbs
salt and pepper
parsley sprigs, to garnish

extremely easy

serves 4

15–20 minutes

1 hour 5 minutes

VARIATION
If herrings are
unavailable, substitute
mackerel or sardines.

❶ Mix the mustard with 25 g/1 oz of the butter until smooth. Spread this mixture over the cut sides of the herring fillets. Season the fillets and roll them up. Set aside. Grease a 2.2 litre/4 pint pie dish with some of the remaining butter.

❷ Slice the potatoes thinly, using a mandolin if possible. Blanch for 3 minutes in boiling, salted water until just tender. Drain well, refresh under cold water, and pat dry.

❸ Heat 2 tablespoons of the remaining butter in a frying pan and add the onion. Cook gently for 8–10 minutes until soft but not coloured. Remove from the heat and set aside.

❹ Put half the potato slices into the bottom of the pie dish with some seasoning, then add half the apple and half the onion. Put the herring fillets on top of the onion and sprinkle with the sage. Repeat the layers in reverse order, ending with potato. Season well and add enough hot stock to reach halfway up the sides of the dish.

❺ Melt the remaining butter and stir in the breadcrumbs until well combined. Sprinkle the breadcrumbs over the pie. Bake in a preheated oven, at 190°C/375° F/Gas Mark 5, for 40–50 minutes until the breadcrumbs are golden and the herrings are cooked through. Serve the pie while it is hot, garnished with parsley.

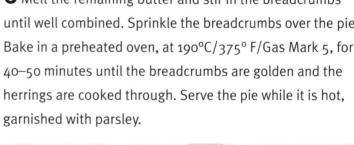

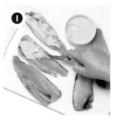

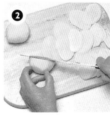

Luxury Fish Pie

85 g/3 oz butter
3 shallots, chopped
15 g/4 oz button
  mushrooms, halved
2 tbsp dry white wine
900 g/2 lb live mussels,
  scrubbed and bearded
600 ml/1 pint vegetable
  stock
300 g/10½ oz monkfish
  fillet, cubed
300 g/10½ oz skinless
  cod fillet, cubed
300 g/10½ oz skinless
  lemon sole
  fillet, cubed
115 g/4 oz tiger prawns,
  peeled
2½ tbsp plain flour
3 tbsp double cream

POTATO TOPPING
1.5 kg/3 lb 5oz floury
  potatoes, cubed
40 g/1½ oz butter
2 egg yolks
125 ml/4 fl oz milk
pinch freshly grated
  nutmeg
salt and pepper
fresh parsley, to garnish

❶ Melt 25 g/1 oz of the butter in a pan, add the shallots, and cook until soft. Add the mushrooms and cook for 2 minutes. Add the wine and simmer until it has evaporated. Transfer to a 1.5 litre/2 pint shallow ovenproof dish, and set aside.

❷ Put the mussels into a saucepan, cover, and heat for 3–4 minutes. Discard any that remain closed. Drain, reserving the cooking liquid. When cool enough to handle, remove the mussels from their shells and add to the mushrooms.

❸ Bring the vegetable stock to the boil, add the monkfish and poach for 2 minutes. Add the cod, sole and prawns and poach for 2 minutes. Add to the mussels and mushrooms.

❹ Melt the remaining butter in a saucepan, add the flour, stir until smooth, and cook for 2 minutes. Stir in the stock and mussel liquid gradually. Add the cream and simmer for 15 minutes, stirring. Season, and pour over the fish.

❺ To make the topping, boil the potatoes for 15–20 minutes until tender. Drain well and mash with the butter, egg, milk, nutmeg and seasoning. Pipe over the fish.

❻ Bake the pie in a preheated oven at 200°C/400°F/Gas Mark 6, for 30 minutes. Serve hot, garnished with parsley.

very easy

serves 4

10 minutes

1 hour
10 minutes

Potato-topped Cod

60 g/2 oz butter
4 waxy potatoes, sliced
1 large onion,
    chopped finely
1 tsp wholegrain
    mustard
1 tsp garam masala
pinch of chilli powder
1 tbsp chopped fresh dill
75 g/2¾ oz fresh
    breadcrumbs
4 cod fillets, about
    175 g/6 oz each
50 g/1¾ oz Gruyère
    cheese, grated
salt and pepper
fresh dill sprigs, to
    garnish

 very easy

serves 4

5–10 minutes

35 minutes

❶ Melt half of the butter in a frying pan. Add the potatoes and fry for 5 minutes, turning until they are browned all over. Remove the potatoes from the pan with a perforated spoon, transfer to a plate, and set aside.

❷ Add the remaining butter to the frying pan and stir in the onion, mustard, garam masala, chilli powder, chopped dill and breadcrumbs. Cook for 2 minutes, stirring constantly to mix the ingredients.

❸ Layer half of the potatoes in the base of an ovenproof dish and place the cod fillets on top. Cover the cod fillets with the remainder of the potato slices. Season to taste with salt and pepper.

❹ Spoon the spicy mixture from the frying pan over the potato, and sprinkle with the grated cheese.

❺ Cook in a preheated oven, 200°C/400°F/Gas Mark 6, for 20–25 minutes, or until the topping is golden and crisp, and the fish is cooked through. Garnish the dish with fresh dill sprigs, and serve at once.

COOK'S TIP
This dish is ideal served with vegetables which can be baked in the oven at the same time.

Layered Fish & Potato Pie

900 g/2 lb waxy potatoes, sliced
60 g/2 oz butter
1 red onion, halved and sliced
50 g/1¾ oz plain flour
450 ml/¾ pint milk
150 ml/5 fl oz double cream
225 g/8 oz smoked haddock fillet, cubed
225 g/8 oz cod fillet, cubed
1 red pepper, diced
125 g/4½ oz broccoli florets
50 g/1¾ oz Parmesan cheese, grated
salt and pepper

 extremely easy

 serves 4

 10 minutes

 55 minutes

COOK'S TIP
Choose your favourite combination of fish, adding salmon or various shellfish for special occasions.

❶ Cook the sliced potatoes in a saucepan of boiling water for 10 minutes. Drain and set aside.

❷ Meanwhile, melt the butter in a saucepan, add the onion and fry gently for 3–4 minutes.

❸ Add the flour and cook for 1 minute. Blend in the milk and cream and bring to the boil, stirring until the sauce is smooth and has thickened.

❹ Arrange half of the potato slices in the base of a shallow ovenproof dish.

❺ Add the fish, diced pepper and broccoli to the sauce and cook over a low heat for 10 minutes. Season with salt and pepper, then spoon the mixture over the layer of potato slices in the dish.

❻ Arrange the remaining potato slices in a layer over the fish mixture. Sprinkle the Parmesan cheese over the top.

❼ Cook in a preheated oven, 180°C/350°F/Gas Mark 4, for 30 minutes or until the potatoes are cooked and the top of the pie is golden.

Potato, Tuna & Cheese Quiche

INGREDIENTS

450 g/1 lb floury potatoes, diced
25 g/1 oz butter
6 tbsp plain flour

FILLING
1 tbsp vegetable oil
1 shallot, chopped
1 garlic clove, crushed
1 red pepper, diced
175 g/6 oz canned tuna in brine, drained
50 g/1¾ oz canned sweetcorn, drained
150 ml/5 fl oz milk
3 eggs, beaten
1 tbsp chopped fresh dill
50 g/1¾ oz mature cheese, grated
salt and pepper

TO GARNISH
fresh dill sprigs
lemon wedges

❶ Cook the potatoes in a pan of boiling water for 10 minutes or until tender. Drain and mash the potatoes. Add the butter and flour and mix to form a dough.

❷ Knead the potato dough on a floured surface to mix it thoroughly, and press the mixture into a 20 cm/8 in flan tin. Prick the base with a fork. Line with greaseproof paper and baking beans, and bake blind in a preheated oven, 200°C/400°F/ Gas Mark 6, for 20 minutes.

❸ Heat the oil in a frying pan, add the shallot, garlic and pepper, and fry gently for 5 minutes. Drain well and spoon into the flan case. Flake the tuna and arrange it over the top with the sweetcorn.

❹ Pour the milk into a bowl, add the eggs and chopped dill, and mix well. Season with salt and pepper.

❺ Pour the egg and dill mixture into the flan case, then sprinkle the grated cheese on top.

❻ Bake in the oven for 20 minutes or until the filling has set. Garnish the quiche with fresh dill sprigs and lemon wedges. Serve with mixed vegetables or salad.

easy

serves 4

20 minutes

1 hour

Vegetable Hotpot

INGREDIENTS

*2 large potatoes,
    sliced thinly*
2 tbsp vegetable oil
*1 red onion, halved and
    sliced*
1 leek, sliced
2 garlic cloves, crushed
1 carrot, cut into chunks
*100 g / 3½ oz broccoli
    florets*
*100 g / 3½ oz cauliflower
    florets*
*2 small turnips,
    quartered*
1 tbsp plain flour
*700 ml / 1¼ pints
    vegetable stock*
150 ml / 5 fl oz dry cider
1 eating apple, sliced
2 tbsp chopped sage
pinch of cayenne pepper
*50 g / 1¾ oz Cheddar
    cheese, grated*
salt and pepper

❶ Cook the potato slices in a saucepan of boiling water for 10 minutes. Drain thoroughly and reserve.

❷ Heat the oil in a large saucepan, add the onion, leek and garlic, and sauté for 2–3 minutes, stirring occasionally. Add the remaining vegetables and sauté for another 3–4 minutes, stirring.

❸ Stir in the flour and cook for 1 minute. Add the stock and cider little by little, and bring to the boil. Add the apple, sage and cayenne pepper, and season well. Remove the pan from the heat. Transfer the vegetables to an ovenproof dish.

❹ Arrange the potato slices on top of the vegetable mixture, covering it completely.

❺ Sprinkle the cheese on top of the potato slices and cook in a preheated oven, 190°C / 375°F / Gas Mark 5, for 30–35 minutes or until the potato is golden brown and beginning to brown slightly around the edges. Serve immediately.

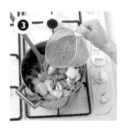

extremely easy

serves 4

25 minutes

1 hour

Cauliflower Bake

INGREDIENTS

450 g / 1 lb cauliflower,
broken into florets
2 large potatoes, cubed
100 g / 3½ oz cherry
tomatoes

SAUCE
25 g / 1 oz butter or
margarine
1 leek, sliced
1 garlic clove, crushed
25 g / 1 oz plain flour
300 ml / 10 fl oz milk
75 g / 2¾ oz mixed
cheeses, such as
Cheddar, Parmesan
or Gruyère, grated
½ tsp paprika
2 tbsp chopped
flat-leaved parsley
salt and pepper
chopped fresh parsley,
to garnish

❶ Cook the cauliflower in a saucepan of boiling water for 10 minutes. Drain well and reserve. Meanwhile, cook the potatoes in a pan of salted boiling water for 10 minutes, drain, and reserve.

❷ To make the sauce, melt the butter or margarine in a saucepan and sauté the leek and garlic for 1 minute. Add the flour and cook, stirring constantly, for 1 minute. Remove the pan from the heat and stir in the milk with 50 g / 1¾ oz of the grated cheeses, the paprika and the parsley, a little at a time. Return the pan to the heat and bring to the boil, stirring constantly. Season with salt and pepper to taste.

❸ Spoon the cauliflower into a deep ovenproof dish. Add the cherry tomatoes and top with the potatoes. Pour the sauce over the potatoes and sprinkle the remaining grated cheeses over the top.

❹ Bake in a preheated oven, 180°C / 350°F / Gas Mark 4, for 20 minutes or until the vegetables are cooked through and the cheese is golden brown and bubbling. Garnish the dish with chopped fresh parsley, and serve immediately.

extremely easy

serves 4

10 minutes

40 minutes

Potato-topped Vegetables in Wine

1 carrot, diced
175 g/6 oz cauliflower
*   florets*
175 g/6 oz broccoli
*   florets*
1 fennel bulb, sliced
75 g/2¾ oz French
*   beans, halved*
25 g/1 oz butter
25 g/1 oz plain flour
150 ml/ 5 fl oz
*   vegetable stock*
150 ml/ 5 fl oz dry
*   white wine*
150 ml/5 fl oz milk
175 g/6 oz chestnut
*   mushrooms,*
*   quartered*
2 tbsp chopped
*   fresh sage*

TOPPING
4 floury potatoes, diced
25 g/1 oz butter
4 tbsp natural yogurt
70 g/2½ oz freshly
*   grated Parmesan*
*   cheese*
1 tsp fennel seeds
salt and pepper

❶ Cook the carrot, cauliflower, broccoli, fennel and beans in a saucepan of boiling water for 10 minutes, or until just tender. Drain the vegetables thoroughly and set aside.

❷ Melt the butter in a saucepan and stir in the flour. Cook for 1 minute, then remove from the heat. Stir in the stock, wine and milk, and bring to the boil, stirring until thickened. Stir in the reserved vegetables, mushrooms and sage.

❸ Meanwhile, make the topping. Cook the diced potatoes in a separate pan of boiling water for 10–15 minutes or until cooked through. Drain the potatoes and mash with the butter, yogurt and half of the cheese. Stir the fennel seeds into the mixture.

❹ Spoon the vegetable mixture into a 1 litre/1¾ pint pie dish. Spoon the potato over the top, or pipe it using a piping bag, covering the filling completely. Sprinkle the remaining cheese on top. Cook in a preheated oven, 190°C/375°F/Gas Mark 5, for 30–35 minutes or until the topping is golden. Serve the dish piping hot.

 very easy

 serves 4

 20 minutes

1 hour
15 minutes

Nutty Harvest Loaf

INGREDIENTS

450 g/1 lb floury
  potatoes, diced
25 g/1 oz butter
1 onion, chopped
2 garlic cloves, crushed
125 g/4½ oz unsalted
  peanuts
75 g/2¾ oz fresh white
  breadcrumbs
1 egg, beaten
2 tbsp chopped fresh
  coriander
150 ml/5 fl oz
  vegetable stock
75 g/2¾ oz closed cap
  mushrooms, sliced
50 g/1¾ oz sun-dried
  tomatoes, sliced
salt and pepper

SAUCE
150 ml/5 fl oz crème
  fraîche
2 tsp tomato purée
2 tsp clear honey
2 tbsp chopped fresh
  coriander

❶ Grease a 450 g/1 lb loaf tin. Boil the potatoes in a saucepan of water for 10 minutes until cooked through. Drain well, then mash and set aside.

❷ Melt half of the butter in a frying pan. Add the onion and garlic and fry gently for 2–3 minutes until soft. Set aside. Chop the nuts finely, or blend them in a food processor for 30 seconds with the breadcrumbs.

❸ Mix the chopped nuts and breadcrumbs into the potatoes with the egg, coriander and vegetable stock. Stir in the onion and garlic, and mix well.

❹ Melt the remaining butter in the frying pan, add the sliced mushrooms, and cook for 2–3 minutes.

❺ Press half of the potato mixture into the base of the loaf tin. Spoon the mushrooms over the potato, and sprinkle the sun-dried tomatoes over them. Spoon the remaining potato mixture on top and smooth the surface. Cover the tin with foil and bake the loaf in a preheated oven, 190°C/350°F/ Gas Mark 5, for 1 hour, or until firm to the touch.

❻ Meanwhile, mix the sauce ingredients together. Cut the loaf into slices and serve them warm with the sauce.

very easy

serves 4

20 minutes

1 hour
20 minutes

Light Meals, Side Dishes & Salads

Light dishes also need to be filling and satisfying, and potato dishes are ideal. Tuna Fish Cakes, served with a simple home-made tomato sauce, are popular with adults and children, and need only a salad garnish to make an attractive meal. A tomato sauce is also served with Sweet Potato Cakes, but in this dish it has the spicy flavours of Thai cooking – garlic, ginger, lime juice and coriander. The recipes in this section include Spain's versatile snack, the *tortilla de patatas* or potato omelette, ideal for a picnic, and crisp Prawn Röstis with Cherry Tomato Salsa.

Spanish Tortilla

INGREDIENTS

100 ml/3½ fl oz olive oil
550 g/1 lb 4 oz
  potatoes, sliced
1 large onion, sliced
1 large garlic clove,
  crushed
6 large eggs
salt and pepper

❶ Heat a 25 cm/10 inch frying pan, preferably non-stick, over a high heat. Pour in the oil and heat. Lower the heat, add the potatoes, onion and garlic. Cook for 15–20 minutes, stirring frequently, until the potatoes are tender.

❷ Beat the eggs in a large bowl and season with salt and pepper. Using a slotted spoon, transfer the potatoes and onion to the bowl of eggs. Pour the excess oil left in the frying pan into a heatproof jug, then scrape the pan.

❸ Add 2 tablespoons of the reserved oil to the pan and reheat. Pour in the potato mixture, smoothing the vegetables into an even layer. Cook for about 5 minutes, shaking the pan occasionally, or until the base is set.

❹ Loosen the sides of the tortilla with a spatula. Place a large plate over the pan, and invert the tortilla onto it.

❺ Add 1 tablespoon of the reserved oil to the pan, reheat it briefly, slide the tortilla gently back into the pan, cooked-side up. Use the spatula to press the sides down. Continue cooking over medium heat for 3–5 minutes until set.

❻ Slide the tortilla onto a serving plate. Let it cool for at least 5 minutes before cutting.

extremely easy

serves 4

10 minutes

40 minutes,
plus 5 minutes
to stand

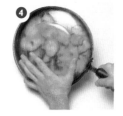

Spicy Potato & Rice Pilaf

INGREDIENTS

200 g/7 oz basmati rice, soaked in cold water for 20 minutes
2 tbsp vegetable oil
½–¾ tsp cumin seeds
225 g/8 oz potatoes, cut into 1 cm/½ inch pieces
225 g/8 oz frozen peas, defrosted
1 green chilli, deseeded and sliced thinly (optional)
½ tsp salt
1 tsp garam masala
½ tsp ground turmeric
¼ tsp cayenne pepper
600 ml/1 pint water
2 tbsp chopped fresh coriander
1 red onion, chopped finely
natural yogurt, to serve

❶ Rinse the soaked rice under cold running water until the water runs clear, then drain and set aside.

❷ Heat the oil in a large, heavy-based saucepan over a medium–high heat. Add the cumin seeds and stir for about 10 seconds until the seeds jump and colour.

❸ Add the potatoes, peas, and chilli, if using, and stir-fry for about 3 minutes until the potatoes just begin to soften.

❹ Add the rice and cook, stirring frequently, until it turns translucent. Stir in the salt, garam masala, turmeric and cayenne pepper, and the water. Bring to the boil, stirring once or twice, then reduce the heat and simmer, covered, until steam holes cover the surface. Do not stir.

❺ Reduce the heat to very low and, if possible, rest the pan on a ring to raise it about 2.5 cm/1 inch above the heat. Cover and steam for about 10 minutes. Remove from the heat, take off the lid, and cover the rice with kitchen paper, then recover and leave the pan to stand for 5 minutes.

❻ Transfer the pilaf gently into a warmed serving bowl and sprinkle with coriander and onion. Serve hot, with yogurt.

 very easy

 serves 4

 15 minutes

 30 minutes, plus 5 minutes to stand

Potatoes in Green Sauce

INGREDIENTS

1 kg/2 lb 4 oz small
waxy potatoes,
peeled
1 onion, halved and
unpeeled
8 garlic cloves,
unpeeled
1 fresh green chilli
8 tomatillos, outer
husks removed, or
small tart tomatoes
225 ml/8 fl oz chicken,
meat or vegetable
stock
½ tsp ground cumin
1 sprig fresh thyme
or generous pinch
dried thyme
1 sprig fresh oregano
or generous pinch
dried oregano
2 tbsp vegetable or
extra-virgin
olive oil
1 courgette, chopped
roughly
1 bunch coriander,
chopped
salt

❶ Put the potatoes in a pan of salted water. Bring to the boil and cook for about 15 minutes or until almost tender. Do not over-cook them. Drain and set aside.

❷ Meanwhile, char the onion, garlic, chilli and tomatillos or tomatoes lightly in a heavy-based, ungreased frying pan. Set aside, and when cool, peel and chop the onion, garlic and chilli, and chop the tomatillos. Put the vegetables in a blender or a food processor with half the stock, and process to a purée. Add the cumin, thyme, and oregano.

❸ Heat the oil in a heavy-based frying pan. Add the purée and cook over a medium heat for about 5 minutes, stirring, to reduce slightly and concentrate the flavours.

❹ Add the potatoes and courgette to the purée and pour in the rest of the stock. Add about half the coriander and cook for 5–10 minutes until the courgette is tender.

❺ Transfer the vegetables to a serving bowl and serve sprinkled with the remaining coriander.

 extremely easy

 serves 4

 15 minutes

 45 minutes

Potatoes with Goat's Cheese & Chipotle Cream

INGREDIENTS

1.25 kg/2 lb 12 oz
  baking potatoes,
  peeled and cut into
  chunks
pinch of salt
pinch of sugar
200 ml/7 fl oz crème
  fraîche
125 ml/4 fl oz vegetable
  or chicken stock
3 garlic cloves, chopped
  finely
a few shakes of bottled
  chipotle salsa, or
  ½ dried chipotle chilli,
  reconstituted,
  deseeded and sliced
  thinly
225 g/8 oz goat's
  cheese, sliced
175 g/6 oz mozzarella
  or Cheddar cheese,
  grated
50 g/1¾ oz Parmesan
  or pecorino cheese,
  grated
salt

❶ Put the potatoes in a pan of water with the salt and sugar. Bring to the boil and cook for about 10 minutes until they are half cooked.

❷ Combine the crème fraîche with the stock, garlic and the chipotle salsa or sliced chipotle chilli.

❸ Arrange half the potatoes in a casserole. Pour half the crème fraîche sauce over the potatoes and cover with the goat's cheese. Top with the remaining potatoes and sauce.

❹ Sprinkle with the grated mozzarella or Cheddar cheese, then with the grated Parmesan or pecorino.

❺ Bake in a preheated oven at 180°C/350°F/Gas Mark 4 for 10 minutes or until the potatoes are tender and the cheese topping is lightly golden. Serve immediately.

 extremely easy

 serves 4

 15 minutes

 20 minutes

Tuna Fish Cakes

INGREDIENTS

225 g/8 oz potatoes,
cubed
1 tbsp olive oil
1 large shallot, chopped
finely
1 garlic clove, chopped
finely
1 tsp thyme leaves
400 g/7 oz canned tuna
in olive oil, drained
grated rind of ½ lemon
1 tbsp chopped fresh
parsley
2–3 tbsp plain flour
1 egg, beaten lightly
115 g/4 oz fresh
breadcrumbs
vegetable oil, for frying
salt and pepper

QUICK TOMATO
SAUCE
2 tbsp olive oil
400 g/14 oz canned
chopped tomatoes
1 garlic clove, crushed
½ tsp sugar
grated rind ½ lemon
1 tbsp chopped fresh
basil
salt and pepper

❶ For the tuna fish cakes, cook the potatoes in plenty of boiling salted water for 12–15 minutes until tender. Transfer to a bowl and mash, leaving a few lumps. Set aside.

❷ Heat the oil in a frying pan and cook the shallot gently for 5 minutes until it is softened. Add the garlic and thyme leaves, and cook for another minute. Allow to cool slightly, then add to the potatoes with the tuna, lemon rind, parsley and seasoning. Mix together well but not too smoothly.

❸ Form the mixture into 6–8 cakes. Dip the cakes first in the flour, then into the egg and finally into the breadcrumbs to coat. Refrigerate for 30 minutes.

❹ Meanwhile, make the tomato sauce. Put the olive oil, tomatoes, garlic, sugar, lemon rind, basil, and seasoning into a saucepan and bring to the boil. Cover and simmer gently for 30 minutes. Uncover and simmer for an additional 15 minutes until thickened.

❺ Heat enough oil in a frying pan to cover the bottom generously. When hot, add the fish cakes in batches, and fry for 3–4 minutes each side until golden and crisp. Drain on kitchen paper while you fry the remaining fish cakes. Serve hot with the tomato sauce.

 very easy

 serves 4

 5 minutes

1 hour
10 minutes

Prawn Röstis

INGREDIENTS

350 g/12 oz potatoes
350 g/12 oz celeriac
1 carrot
½ small onion
225 g/8 oz cooked
  peeled prawns,
  thawed if frozen
  and well drained
  on kitchen paper
2½ tbsp plain flour
1 egg, beaten lightly
vegetable oil, for frying
salt and pepper

CHERRY TOMATO
SALSA
225 g/8 oz mixed cherry
  tomatoes, quartered
½ small mango,
  diced finely
1 red chilli, deseeded
  and chopped finely
½ small red onion,
  chopped finely
1 tbsp chopped
  coriander
1 tbsp chopped fresh
  chives
2 tbsp olive oil
2 tsp lemon juice
salt and pepper

❶ For the salsa, mix the tomatoes, mango, chilli, red onion, coriander, chives, olive oil, lemon juice and seasoning. Set aside to allow the flavours to infuse.

❷ Using a food processor or the fine blade of a box grater, grate the potatoes, celeriac, carrot and onion finely. Mix the grated vegetables with the prawns, flour and egg, then season well with salt and pepper and set aside.

❸ Divide the prawn mixture into 8 equal pieces. Press each into a greased 10 cm/4 inch cutter (if you only have 1 cutter, shape the röstis individually).

❹ In a large frying pan, heat a shallow layer of oil. When hot, transfer the vegetable cakes, still in the cutters, to the frying pan, in four batches if necessary. When the oil sizzles underneath, remove the cutter. Fry gently, pressing down with a spatula, for 6–8 minutes on each side, until the röstis are crisp and browned and the vegetables are tender. Drain on kitchen paper. Serve the röstis immediately, while still hot, accompanied by the tomato salsa.

 very easy

 serves 4

 10 minutes

 1 hour

Salt Cod Hash

INGREDIENTS

750 g/1 lb 10 oz salt cod
4 eggs
3 tbsp olive oil, plus extra for drizzling
8 rashers rindless smoked streaky bacon, chopped
700 g/1 lb 9 oz old potatoes, diced
8 garlic cloves
8 thick slices good-quality white bread
2 plum tomatoes, skinned and chopped
2 tsp red wine vinegar
2 tbsp chopped fresh parsley, plus extra to garnish
salt and pepper
lemon wedges, to garnish

❶ Soak the salt cod in cold water for 2 hours. Drain well. Discard the soaking water. Bring a large saucepan of water to the boil and add the fish. Remove from the heat and leave to stand for 10 minutes. Drain the fish on kitchen paper and flake the flesh. Set aside.

❷ Bring a saucepan of water to the boil and add the eggs. Simmer for 7 minutes from when the water boils for a soft centre, 9 minutes for a firm centre. Drain the eggs and plunge them into cold water to stop them cooking. When cool, shell the eggs and chop them coarsely. Set aside.

❸ Heat the oil in a large frying pan and add the bacon. Cook over a medium heat for 4–5 minutes until crisp and brown. Remove with a slotted spoon and drain on kitchen paper. Add the potatoes to the pan with the garlic, and cook over a medium heat for 8–10 minutes until crisp.

❹ Meanwhile, toast the bread on both sides until golden. Drizzle with olive oil and set aside.

❺ Add the tomatoes, bacon, fish, vinegar, and chopped egg to the potatoes and garlic. Cook for 2 minutes. Stir in the parsley and season to taste. Put the toast on plates, top with the hash, and serve with parsley and lemon wedges.

 easy

 serves 4

 10 minutes, plus 2 hours to soak and 10 minutes to stand

30 minutes

Potatoes in Creamed Coconut

INGREDIENTS

600 g/1 lb 5 oz potatoes
1 onion, sliced thinly
2 red bird's eye chillies,
   chopped
½ tsp salt
½ tsp ground black
   pepper
85 g/3 oz creamed
   coconut
350 ml/12 fl oz
   vegetable or
   chicken stock
chopped fresh
   coriander or basil,
   to garnish

❶ Peel the potatoes and cut into 2 cm/¾ inch chunks.

❷ Place the potatoes in a pan with the onion, chilli, salt, pepper and creamed coconut. Stir in the stock.

❸ Bring to the boil, stirring, then lower the heat, cover, and simmer gently, stirring occasionally, until the potatoes are tender.

❹ Adjust the seasoning to taste, then sprinkle the potatoes with chopped coriander or basil. Serve hot.

 extremely easy

 serves 4

 10 minutes

 15 minutes

COOK'S TIP

If the potatoes are a thin-skinned or new variety, wash or scrub them and cook them in their skins. This adds dietary fibre and nutrients to the dish, and cuts preparation time. Cook baby new potatoes whole.

Potatoes & Spinach in Yellow Curry Sauce

INGREDIENTS

2 garlic cloves, chopped
3 cm/1¼ inch piece
  galangal, chopped
1 lemon grass stem,
  chopped finely
1 tsp coriander seeds
3 tbsp vegetable oil
2 tsp red curry paste
½ tsp turmeric
200 ml/7 fl oz coconut
  milk
250 g/9 oz potatoes,
  peeled and cut into
  2 cm/ ¾ inch cubes
100 ml/3½ oz vegetable
  stock
200 g/7 oz young
  spinach leaves
1 small onion, sliced
  thinly into rings

 extremely easy

serves 4

5 minutes

15 minutes

❶ Place the garlic, galangal, lemon grass and coriander seeds in a mortar and pound with a pestle until a smooth paste forms.

❷ Heat 2 tablespoons of the oil in a frying pan or a wok. Stir in the paste and stir-fry for 30 seconds. Stir in the Thai red curry paste and turmeric, then add the coconut milk and bring to the boil.

❸ Add the potatoes and stock. Return to the boil, then lower the heat and simmer, uncovered, for 10–12 minutes until the potatoes are almost tender.

❹ Stir in the spinach and simmer until the leaves wilt.

❺ Meanwhile, fry the onion rings in the remaining oil until they are crisp and golden brown. Arrange them on top of the curry just before serving.

COOK'S TIP
Choose a firm, waxy potato for this dish, one that will keep its shape during cooking, rather than a floury variety which breaks up during cooking.

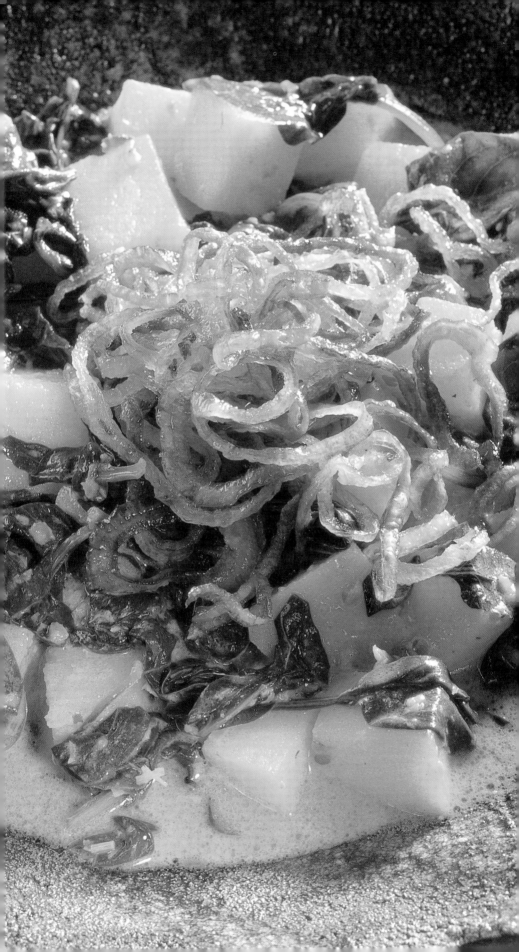

Sweet Potato Cakes with Soy & Tomato Sauce

INGREDIENTS

2 sweet potatoes
(500 g/ 1 lb 2 oz
total weight)
2 garlic cloves, crushed
1 small green chilli,
chopped
2 sprigs coriander,
chopped
1 tbsp dark soy sauce
plain flour, for shaping
vegetable oil, for frying
sesame seeds, for
sprinkling

SOY & TOMATO
SAUCE
2 tsp vegetable oil
1 garlic clove, chopped
finely
¾ inch piece fresh
ginger root,
chopped finely
3 tomatoes, skinned
and chopped
2 tbsp dark soy sauce
1 tbsp lime juice
2 tbsp chopped fresh
coriander

❶ First make the sauce. Heat the oil in a wok and stir-fry the garlic and ginger for about 1 minute. Add the tomatoes and stir-fry for another 2 minutes. Remove from the heat and stir in the soy sauce, lime juice and coriander. Set aside and keep warm.

❷ Peel the sweet potatoes and grate finely (you can do this quickly in a food processor). Place the garlic, chilli, and coriander in a mortar and crush with a pestle to a paste. Stir in the soy sauce, and mix with the sweet potatoes.

❸ Divide the mixture into 12 equal portions and shape each with your hands into a flat, round patty shape. Dip each portion into flour and pat into shape.

❹ Heat a shallow layer of oil in a wide frying pan. Fry the potato cakes over a high heat until they are golden, turning once. Drain on kitchen paper and sprinkle with sesame seeds. Serve hot, with a spoonful of the sauce.

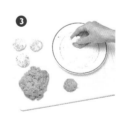

 extremely easy

 serves 4

 10–15 minutes

 15 minutes

Sweet Potato & Banana Salad

INGREDIENTS

450 g/1 lb sweet
    potatoes, diced
50 g/1¾ oz butter
1 tbsp lemon juice
1 garlic clove, crushed
1 red pepper, deseeded
    and diced
1 green pepper,
    deseeded and diced
2 bananas, sliced thickly
2 thick slices white
    bread, crusts
    removed, diced
salt and pepper

DRESSING
2 tbsp clear honey
2 tbsp chopped chives
2 tbsp lemon juice
2 tbsp olive oil

 extremely easy

 serves 4

 15 minutes

 20 minutes

① Cook the sweet potatoes in a saucepan of boiling water for 10–15 minutes, or until tender. Drain thoroughly and set aside for later use.

② Meanwhile, melt the butter in a frying pan. Add the lemon juice, garlic and peppers, and cook for 3 minutes, turning constantly.

③ Add the banana slices to the pan and cook for 1 minute. Remove the bananas from the pan with a slotted spoon and stir them into the potatoes.

④ Add the bread cubes to the frying pan and fry for 2 minutes, turning frequently, until they are golden brown on all sides.

⑤ Mix the dressing ingredients in a small saucepan and warm them gently until the honey is runny.

⑥ Spoon the potato mixture into a serving dish and season to taste with salt and pepper. Pour the dressing over the potatoes and sprinkle the fried croûtons over the top. Serve the salad immediately, while still warm.

VARIATION
Use firm, slightly underripe bananas in this recipe. They will not turn soft and mushy when fried.

Indian Potato Salad

INGREDIENTS

4 medium floury
   potatoes (900 g/
   2 lb weight), diced
75 g/2¾ oz small
   broccoli florets
1 small mango, diced
4 spring onions, sliced
salt and pepper

DRESSING
½ tsp ground cumin
½ tsp ground coriander
1 tbsp mango chutney
150 ml/5 fl oz
   natural yogurt
1 tsp ginger root,
   chopped
2 tbsp chopped fresh
   coriander

 extremely easy

 serves 4

 25 minutes

20 minutes

❶ Cook the potatoes in a saucepan of boiling water for 10 minutes or until tender. Drain and place in a mixing bowl.

❷ Meanwhile, blanch the broccoli florets in a separate saucepan of boiling water for 2 minutes. Drain well and add to the potatoes in the bowl.

❸ When the potatoes and broccoli have cooled, add the diced mango and sliced spring onions. Season to taste with salt and pepper, and mix well to combine.

❹ Place all the dressing ingredients together in a small bowl, and stir well.

❺ Spoon the dressing over the potato mixture and mix carefully, taking care not to break up the potato dice and the broccoli florets.

❻ Serve the salad at once, perhaps accompanied by small, cooked, spiced poppadoms.

COOK'S TIP
Mix the dressing in advance and leave it to chill in the refrigerator for a few hours for a stronger flavour to develop.

Potato, Rocket & Apple Salad

INGREDIENTS

*2 large potatoes (600 g/
 1 lb 5 oz weight)*
*2 green eating apples,
 diced*
1 tsp lemon juice
25 g/1 oz walnut pieces
*125 g/4½ oz goat's
 cheese, cubed*
*150 g/5½ oz rocket
 leaves*
salt and pepper

DRESSING
2 tbsp olive oil
1 tbsp red wine vinegar
1 tsp clear honey
1 tsp fennel seeds

❶ Cook the potatoes unpeeled in a pan of boiling water for 15–20 minutes until tender. Drain and leave to cool. Slice the cooled potatoes and transfer to a serving bowl.

❷ Toss the diced apples in the lemon juice, drain, and stir into the cold potatoes.

❸ Add the walnut pieces, cheese cubes and rocket leaves, then toss the salad to mix.

❹ In a small bowl, whisk the dressing ingredients together and pour the dressing over the salad. Season to taste and serve the salad immediately.

extremely easy

serves 4

5 minutes,
plus 15 minutes
to cool

15 minutes

COOK'S TIP
The apple will discolour
if you delay serving the
salad. Alternatively,
prepare the other
ingredients and add
the apple just as you
are ready to serve.

Potato & Italian Sausage Salad

INGREDIENTS

450 g/1 lb waxy
  potatoes
1 radicchio or lollo rosso
  lettuce
1 green pepper, sliced
175 g/6 oz Italian
  sausage, sliced
1 red onion, halved
  and sliced
125 g/4½ oz sun-dried
  tomatoes, sliced
2 tbsp shredded fresh
  basil

DRESSING
1 tbsp balsamic vinegar
1 tsp tomato purée
2 tbsp olive oil
salt and pepper

❶ Cook the potatoes in a saucepan of boiling water for 20 minutes, or until cooked through. Drain and leave to cool.

❷ Line a large serving plate with the radicchio or lollo rosso lettuce leaves.

❸ Slice the cooled potatoes and arrange them in layers on the lettuce-lined serving plate with the sliced green pepper, sliced Italian sausage, red onion, sun-dried tomatoes and shredded fresh basil.

❹ Put the balsamic vinegar, tomato purée and olive oil together into a small bowl and whisk until combined. Season to taste with salt and pepper. Pour the dressing over the potato salad and serve immediately.

extremely easy

serves 4

25 minutes

25 minutes

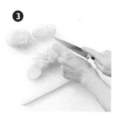

COOK'S TIP
If you buy jars of sun-dried tomatoes in oil, rinse the oil from the tomatoes and pat them dry on paper towels before using.

94